Bad Hair Life

Bad Hair Life

Bad Hair Life

Other Books by Mae Hoover

My First Cookbook

To Climb a Mountain Audio

To Climb a Mountain Print

The Journey to and from the Mountain

Marriage for the Long Haul - e-book

When Your Mama Calls You Mama

The Fleeced Flock

If I Wrote a Book – workbook

Bad Hair Life

BAD HAIR (DAY) LIFE

Mae has written a delightful book about her personal struggles with her hair. It seems all her life her hair has been a "problem." It was thin and lifeless; it couldn't take a perm and the funny stories about dying it make me chuckle even now.   There was the time her mother thought she should have dark eye brows so asked the beautician to dye them black so they would last longer. Mae comments, "People could see my eyebrows approaching long before they saw me." This is a short and delightful book that will keep you

Bad Hair Life

laughing to the end. By the
way, Mae's solution to the
hair problem—hats!
Is it possible that Mae is
writing about more than bad
hair?
Olga Ferris, Retired
education administrator

Mae's struggles with her
hair remind me of my
relationship to various
problematic parts of body. I
have hated most of my
body for my entire life. My
hands and feet are wide
(read ugly.) My thighs and
arms are an absolute
abomination. My hips – well
let's not even go there. But
above all, literally, my bust

Bad Hair Life

is far too big. It attracts way
too much attention and I
don't mean the good kind.
Mae never learned to
appreciate her hair but she
did learn how to cope. She
developed a strategy to
minimize what she felt was
a flaw; a useful skill she can
deploy in any other arenas.
 Deborah Bronson

Bad Hair D~~ay~~ Life

by

Mae Hoover

Cover & art work by Madison Hoover

and Cay Livingston

of ccaysdesigns.com

Mountain Top Books

Fort Worth, Texas

Bad Hair Life

Copyright 2015 Mae Hoover

All rights reserved. This book may
not be duplicated in any form except
as allowed by the U.S. Copyright
Act of 1989, as amended, without
the prior and express written per-
mission of the publisher.

Published by Mountain Top Books
A division of Foundation for
Publication
Fort Worth, Texas

Bad Hair Life

Introduction

The most useful and healthy
single thing I have learned in life
is to have the ability to laugh at
myself. Nothing can be that
serious if you can laugh about it.

Almost everything to me is
funny. I've never taken life
very seriously. Sometimes
it takes me a while to see
the humor, but it's always
there.

While still in elementary
school one of my Sunday
school teachers told us to

go home and figure out
what our talent was. I
stewed all week trying to
figure that out.

I couldn't play the piano. I
couldn't carry a tune in a
bucket. I never won the
track races and I always
came in second in spelling.
My art teacher told me I
didn't have talent in that
area.

What was my talent?

That next Sunday I walked
to church still trying to figure
it out. When it came my

turn I said, "A smile. That's
my talent."

And it was and is my
greatest talent.

Later the smile became
laughter. That's why I call
myself a "laffologist" when I
am speaking. My stories
are true and they make
people laugh.

My hope is that you will laugh as
you read my book. And maybe
you will find things in your life to
laugh about.

Mae Hoover

Bad Hair Life

Bad Hair ~~Day~~ Life

by Mae Hoover

Chapter 1

I didn't just have a bad hair day -- I had a bad hair life!

Hold onto your hats now, as you read about my bad hair.

Before I start, I need to thank God for my bad hair! One of my great grandmothers was totally bald – over 125 years ago! Bald wasn't considered

beautiful in women at that
time.

Born with very blond,
straight, fine thin hair, my
mother did her best to make
me her curly headed doll.
She "rolled" my hair every
night, but by morning the
pins or rollers would be
scattered all over the bed
and my hair would be
straight.

Mother could "roll" my hair
in the morning and not
brush it and it would be
curly and cute until the wind

hit it. It would then be
straight again!

She tried "pig tails" which
made thin little braids.
She'd pull the hair so tight I
couldn't smile before noon,
at which time the hair had

pulled out of the braid and
the ribbons were gone. The
good thing about that is she
pulled all the tenderness out
of my head before I started
to school. It never bothered
me to have some mean little
boy pull my hair. See, all
things do work together for
good.

Bad Hair Life

Then Mother got desperate.
She tried home
permanents. They either
fried my hair, or didn't work.
Once half my hair curled
and the other half remained
straight. Nothing you can
do about that.

Bad Hair Life

Besides, home permanents
had an ugly chemical smell.
I couldn't sleep for a couple
of nights until I got used to
the stink. I don't know how
people around me felt.

Then Mother took me to the
beauty shop where they
hooked me up to this
machine that attached to
each curl they made and
cooked my scalp. It looked
like something Frankenstein
would have used.

I would come out with
blistered scalp, missing hair

and frizzled ends. So much hair broke off at the part that it looked a little like a Mohawk. What was left <u>would</u> be curly for a couple of weeks though.

She "set" my hair every night and every morning for as long as I could remember.

So much for curls.

Bad Hair Life

Chapter 2

I was born right at the end
of World War II. I was
about five years old when
chewing gum became
available. Everyone loved
chewing gum. Supplies of
gum were limited, so when
we got some we guarded
it. When we got tired of
chewing it we'd keep it
somewhere in a safe place
until another time. Most of
us put the wad of gum on
the bedpost at night.

Bad Hair Life

There's a song about that I
think.

My brothers liked to play
tricks on me and I was
gullible. They convinced
me if I put the gum behind
my ear it would stay soft
until I was ready to chew
again. That sounded
logical because it got kind
of hard on the bedpost.

That night I put the gum
behind my ear and went
happily to sleep. In the
morning I was stuck to the
pillow and my hair was

Bad Hair Life

There's a song about that I think.

My brothers liked to play tricks on me and I was gullible. They convinced me if I put the gum behind my ear it would stay soft until I was ready to chew again. That sounded logical because it got kind of hard on the bedpost.

That night I put the gum behind my ear and went happily to sleep. In the morning I was stuck to the pillow and my hair was

24

stuck to itself and my
scalp.

Mother used ice and
everything she could think
of to try to get the stuff out
of my hair, but finally she
had to cut it out. I think
she punished my brothers,
who were thoroughly
enjoying their prank.

Bad Hair Life

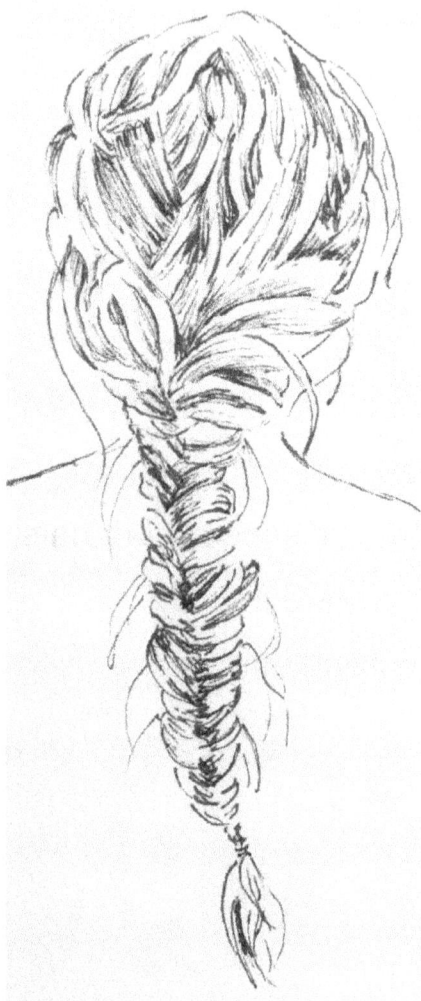

Chapter 3

I decided I had to get out
on my own and away from
that torture of hair curlers
and permanents, etc.!

I began selling donuts
from my uncle's donut
shop to the neighbors. I
was still in elementary
school. I'd take orders,
walk to the shop early in
the morning and deliver to
the customers. I earned
and saved every penny.

Bad Hair Life

I baby-sat when I was old
enough and saved every
penny.

Some day, I reasoned, I'd
have enough money to get
my hair done the way I
wanted it.

Bad Hair Life

Yikes!

Bad Hair Life

Chapter 3

Although I had very little
hair on my head, it grew
down my neck and
became quite long.
Mother would shave my
neck regularly.

I remember one Easter
morning she had pulled
my hair into a pony tail, but
the hair on my neck
needed shaving. My
cousin and her family lived
with us at the time, so

Bad Hair Life

Mother asked Jan to
shave my neck since she
was busy. Jan had a real
ornery streak, but she
promised to do a good job,
and I submitted.

When she got done, I
pulled half my pony tail off
and threw it in the trash.
She had shaved half way
up my ears!

When I was in the seventh
grade, Mother sent me to
the beauty shop to get
another electric head
cooking. I had my own
money this time and I got

all my hair cut off as short
as they could make it.

I thought Mother would get
mad, but she loved it. So
did I. She remembered
the twenties, where girls
wore "boyish bobs."

But all my friends had a
full head of hair, and I had
so little I felt bad.

I bought a fake bun and
wore it on the back of my
head. That looked really
like an old woman. I
bought a "fall" which
looked even worse. After

that I tried a wiglet. I
would pin it in, but the pins
would fall out before the
day was over. Besides I
looked like a little girl trying
to look like an old woman
or maybe even like a
holiness preacher's wife
(Which, of course, I am!).

Bad Hair Life

Bad Hair Life

Chapter 4

In junior high school everyone sprayed colored powder into their hair. I did that too. I must have thought nobody would notice my purple or green hair.

Although I had very little hair on my head and lots on my neck, it began growing on my legs!

Bad Hair Life

Mother warned me not to
shave my legs. She said
she never had and now
she had no hair on her
legs. She insisted if I ever
started shaving I would get
tired someday and my legs
would look like my Aunt
Lillian's. She had black
curly hair on her legs. And
the hairs would stick out
through her nylon hose.

By the way, Mother not
only had no hair on her
legs, she had no eyebrows
or facial hair. I guess she
never shaved there either.

Bad Hair Life

I knew curls on my legs (or
anywhere else) were
unlikely, and in gym I
needed shaved legs. She
may have been right about
never losing the hair on
my legs though. And I did
get tired of shaving. I just
cover my legs with long
pants now that I'm old.

Come to think of it, my
husband never shaved his
legs and now that he's 75
he doesn't have hair there
either.

One of the Redneck
comedians said he keeps

Bad Hair Life

his teen age daughter
away from the boys by
making her wear hose that
have long curly hair on
them.

That would work – if you
could get the daughter to
wear them.

One beautician actually
told me I had plenty of
hair. It was just skinny.

After the summer of my
8th grade year all my
friends came back to
school with bleached

Bad Hair Life

blond hair. That must be
the thing, I thought.

"How did you get that
pretty blond hair?" I asked
them.

"We put lemon juice all
over our hair and lay out in
the sun."

I did that, but all I got was
ants in my hair.

I've always had a problem
in that I believe everything
everyone tells me -- even
if over and over I find out
they are "kidding."

41

Why I thought I should do
anything to my almost
platinum blond hair is now
a mystery to me, but kids
want to fit in.

Finally they admitted to me
they used a product called
"Light and Bright." I
bought some of that and
applied it to my hair
according to directions. I
waited a couple of hours
and could see no change,
so I applied it a second
time. No change, so I
used up the bottle.

Bad Hair Life

The next day I had orange
hair that was frizzed on the
ends.

It took over a year for all
that to grow out.

Bad Hair Life

Chapter 5

Mother always "did" my
hair while I lived at home.
When I went away to
college my roommate "did"
my hair. When I married I
had to learn what to do
with it. Since I'm a slow
learner, it just looked bad
most of the time.

The hair on my head was
very blond and so were my
eye brows. In fact, it
looked like I didn't have
any brows. Mother

decided when I was in the
7th grade I needed to start
"fixing" my face. She
thought it might be too
much to color my brows
with a pencil, so she took
me to the beauty shop to
have them DYED! To
save money she had them
dye me BLACK. That way
it would last a long time!

People could see my
brows coming down the
street before they could
see me!

Because I had my own
money by then I continued

to get them dyed, but a
lighter, more natural color.

I was visiting Jan (that
ornery cousin) when it was
time to get a new dye job.
She convinced me to let
her save me money and
let her do it. That would
save me money. I am a
really slow learner. I
agreed. One of her friends
came over in the middle of
the procedure.

It takes two applications to
complete the color. She
laid the cotton ball on my
nose between the

applications. I objected, but she assured me it was only the first coat and had no color. She lied! She dyed the entire tip of my nose dark brown. I was literally a "brown nose."

You can't scrub that stuff off! It finally wore off on its own after a couple of weeks!

After I married, Alex and I became the house parents of a dormitory at the University of Kansas. There were about 20 boys living there.

Bad Hair Life

Close to the Christmas holidays I mentioned my need to get my brows dyed again. One of the guys said his mother owned a beauty shop and he used to work for her doing that. He would pick up some dye during the holiday and dye my brows for me when he returned.

This was not my cousin after all, and I was always anxious to save a little money, so I agreed.

Bad Hair Life

When we were ready to do the deed, I sat in a chair in the middle of the living room and all the guys gathered around to watch. Apparently the guy lied to me about doing this before. When he finished I looked like Groucho Marx with brows 1/2 inch thick.

"Not to worry," he said, "I can remove it."

And he did -- along with about three layers of my skin.

Then he tried again. This time the dye feathered out in the raw skin making an even worse mess than the original.

"Not to worry," he said, "I can remove it."

And he did -- along with another three or more layers of skin.

I refused to let him try again, besides I think he must have run out of dye by that time.

Bad Hair Life

My forehead and eyelids
peeled clear across my
scalp for months after that.
From that time until this I
use a pencil or a brush to
put on temporary color.

One of my friends had her
brows and eye lids
tattooed, so she wouldn't
have to bother with make-
up. I rejected that idea
completely. I tend to faint
at the sight of a needle.
The sight of one headed
for my eye would be all
she wrote for me.

Chapter 6

I didn't wear make-up in
college (but I did have
dyed eyebrows). My dorm
was close to a fraternity
house. My group and the
frat boys hung out at a
corner drug store and
became friends with each
other. We all attended

dances at the Union
Building and danced
together. Toward the end
of the school year the
fraternity held their annual
Rose Ball. All of my gang
was invited.

I drug out my formal dress,
but my roommate didn't
approve of it. She called a
hall meeting and the gang
decided to "fix" me up.
They found the perfect
gown and then set to work
on my make-up and hair. I
looked gorgeous! If
anyone had touched my

Bad Hair Life

hair it would have felt like
plastic, but it looked great.

We went to the ball
together. Although I loved
dancing and had danced
with most of the guys, no
one asked me to dance. I
became the proverbial wall
flower. When the ball was
drawing to a close I
cornered one of the guys I
knew best and asked him,
"Why am I getting the cold
shoulder here?"

He recognized my voice.
"Mae! Is that you? None
of us knew who you were!"

Bad Hair Life

I went back to being
mousey Mae.

The only way my hair ever
looked decent was in a
short hair cut. An older
lady in our church came to
me one day.

"Honey, didn't you know it
is a sin to "bob" your hair.
God wants your hair to be
your glory," she told me.
Hers was twisted into a
bun on top of her head.

"If God wanted my hair to
be my glory," I told her,

Bad Hair Life

"He'd have given me more
of it."

Bad Hair Life

Chapter 7

Following my graduation
from high school and
Alex's from college we
planned to get married.
He began his junior year at
the University of Kansas
and took a glamorous
photograph of me for his
dresser.

I am photogenic, and I had
gone directly from the
beauty shop to the

photography studio for that
photo.

Alex's dormitory didn't
have dorm parents, and
that year the University
demanded that every
house have dorm parents.
The guys at our house
looked at my photo and
persuaded Alex to marry
me ahead of schedule and
become their dorm
parents.

So it was that we married
and in the heat of August
we drove from Texas to
Kansas for Alex's senior

year. Our old car had no
air conditioning and open
windows don't help any
hair do -- even a good
one.

We no sooner stepped out
of the car when one of the
guys from New York
walked up to me, looked
me up and down, and
said, "They've got good
photographers in Texas."

Regardless of my hair
situation we were in
demand as chaperones on
campus that year.

Bad Hair Life

I could go to the beauty
shop and with lots of hair
spray and gel and back
combing I could look very
glamorous for the entire
day, and the next day -- if I
didn't sleep.

I found one beauty
operator who could do my
hair and it would last a
whole week. Each night I
would wrap my hair in
toilet paper and put a night
bonnet over it. (Like the
cap Aunt Jemima wore on
the early syrup bottles)
Each morning I would un-
wrap myself. I was a little

Bad Hair Life

like that bear on the toilet
paper commercial. I had
little bits of white paper
stuck amidst my "do." I
can't tell you what that get-
up did to my love life!

Then my miracle
beautician got pregnant
and left the business. No
one else ever made a "do"
last more than two days.

I lost my night cap, so I
tried using a shower cap.
Those things are plastic. I
sleep through anything --
including my hair
completely sweating out

and dripping out from
under the shower cap.
When I took the thing off in
the morning the hair spray
that had been applied had
turned into glue and with
the addition of cups of
sweat had adhered my
hair to my scalp in a most
peculiar formation. It was
difficult to get my hair back
into straight clean hair
again.

After several years of
wrestling with it, my hair
began falling out. Big
patches of hair fell out. I
went to a dermatologist.

Bad Hair Life

He said I was allergic to all
the hair care products I
was using. I was to use
only a special soap on it,
and no hair care products.
Also I was to massage a
salve into the scalp twice a
day.

Can you just imagine what
that looked like!

Bad Hair Life

Chapter 8

I bought a wig. That was
wonderful. I could just
take my hair off and put it
on a fake head each night
and pop it back on every
morning looking great --
with more hair than I had
ever had! For the first time
in my life I could be proud
of my hair -- even if it
wasn't mine. Well, I did
own it.

Bad Hair Life

My youngest son toured
the neighborhood daily
and reported to each of
the ladies what everyone
else was doing. I can just
imagine him telling them,
"My mama takes her hair
off at night and puts it on
the dresser."

He went with me to the
department store one day.
The clerk said, "Hello, little
boy. How old are you?"

He answered, "I'm four,
my sister is seven, my
brother is ten, my mama is

thirty and my daddy is
thirty-four."

I shrugged and told the
clerk, "I'm just glad he
doesn't know how much I
weigh."

I found an appropriate
bumper sticker. It read
"God knows the number of
hairs on your head – and
on your wig, too."

Wigs had some drawbacks
though. I had to buy a
second one to wear when
one was being "fixed" at
the beauty shop. I pinned

it in place with bobby pins,
but before long I lost the
hair around the pins, so I
had to just put it on and
hope it stayed.

Once it blew off in an
outdoor shopping mall.
My son ran after it and I
plopped it back on --
backwards! (Not to
mention with a bit of trash
in it). I proudly walked
back to the car ignoring
that the bangs were
tickling my shoulders.

Once I was walking to my
neighbor's house. She

had a tree with a low
hanging branch and
although I ducked under it,
I didn't duck deep enough.
A branch speared my wig
and held it while I walked
away. Thankfully I was
not like Absalom in the
Bible who was hung by his
hair in a tree. I ducked
back under my hair, broke
off the offending twig and
continued my journey,
hoping my neighbor would
think that tree "part" was a
new hair decoration.

My fine hair would straggle
out from under the wigs,

so I let my own hair grow
so I could put it into a wad
and keep it up. It was
almost waist length after
seven years of wearing
wigs. I would twist it up
into that wad on top of my
head and it didn't even
make a bulge in my wig.

Now that's "skinny" hair!

My husband used to give
our sons their hair cuts. I
had watched many times
and it looked simple. Alex
was out of town once
when Tommy needed his
hair cut. I got out the

scissors and briefly
studied the situation. He
had so much hair and it
was getting long. I
decided to cut off as much
as I could, then go back
and even it out. I whacked
it off in chunks – clear to
the scalp in some places.

When Alex came home he
was mortified. Tommy
was only about 3 years old
and he was so
embarrassed he wouldn't
go out without a hat! Alex
forbid me to ever touch the
scissors again.

Bad Hair Life

Alex gave Tommy his first burr haircut.

One July we went on a cruise of the Mediterranean and the Holy Land. We were to go to Egypt and I had heard it could get to 117 degrees there in July. The short wind-blown look of hair had become popular, so I went to a beauty shop and got my hair cut.

Besides, wigs don't pack well. That was the last time I wore a wig.

Bad Hair Life

That first winter I nearly
froze to death without a
wig to keep the heat in.
Not too many years later I
had my age to keep me
warm.

I heard a comedian say
the cause of global
warming is all those baby
boomers having hot
flashes.

Chapter 9

When our youngest son was getting married, he was marrying a girl seven years younger than himself. My hair had begun to turn gray by that time. I didn't want to look like his grandmother, so I asked a beauty operator to put a rinse on my hair to cover the gray. She did and it looked wonderful.

Bad Hair Life

That was several months
before the big date. When
it was the week of the
wedding I returned to the
shop.

I imagined she had kept a
record of what she did to
make my hair such a
natural color.

I was wrong.

Whatever she did the
second time turned my
hair green! Oh, not a
shamrock green, but in
sunlight or florescent light

-- like in the church -- it
was definitely green.

When I returned home I
went back to the beauty
shop to get her to "fix" my
hair. She refused to do
anything about it.

I went to another shop and
discovered the "rinse" was
actually a dye. Hair the
natural ash color of mine is
often turned green with
dye. That shop agreed to
dye it again to cover the
green. Then it was red.

Bad Hair Life

After that I decided to let
God color my hair
whatever color <u>He</u> chose.

Two weeks after Andy's
wedding we attended his
graduation from medical
school.

The beauty operator who
dyed my hair red sold me
a round plastic bristle
brush with little balls on
the tip of each bristle. She
told me to roll a chunk of
hair on the round brush
and use a hair dryer to
make it last as a curl.

Bad Hair Life

I tried that in the hotel getting ready to attend Andy's graduation. That was when I still had red hair. Andy and his new wife were in an adjoining room. Somehow the little balls on that brush picked up hair that I didn't intend to pick up and rolled it into the hair I did intend to pick up. The result was knotted hair and a brush locked onto my scalp.

My husband, Alex, has no patience with stuff like that. He probably would have given up and yanked

out the hank of hair with
the brush. Andy, on the
other hand, has the
patience of Job and the
skill of a surgeon with
knots.

I thought about just leaving
the brush there and
pretending it was a new
hair ornament. I know
some black men who go
around with big combs in
their hair. It looks pretty
cool. Maybe my brush
would look cool.

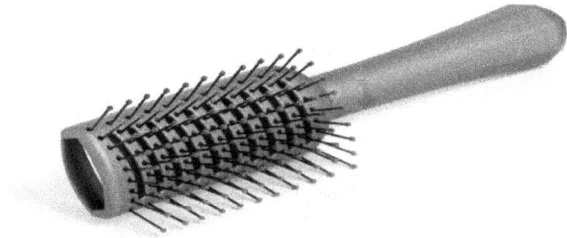

Andy thought not and he painstakingly removed the brush hair by hair, and I was able to attend the graduation ... with straight hair.

The brush went into the trash.

Bad Hair Life

Chapter 10

After the failures of the
other beauty shops to
meet my expectations I
needed another place. I
noticed there was a shop
across the street from our
town house. I walked over
one Saturday for a hair
cut.

I was the only Caucasian
customer. The place was
packed. People had Z's
shaved into their hair;
some had corn rows;

some had dread locks. It was interesting.

The beautician put me in her chair and turned me away from the mirror, so I was unable to see what she was doing to me. She started at my neckline, cut the hair, curled it with a curling iron, and sprayed it. Then she proceeded to the row of hair just above the finished row. She continued until my whole head was finished to her satisfaction.

Bad Hair Life

I had quite an audience
during the procedure.
Making conversation I
asked, "Do you give
permanents here?"

"Yes," she said.

"How much do they cost?"

"I don't know. We've
never given one."

Her clientele got their hair
straightened -- not curled.

My hair was beautiful
when she turned me
around toward the mirror.

Bad Hair Life

I was pleased with the
result, but a bit too
uncomfortable to return. I
certainly understand how
black people feel when
surrounded by us --
especially if we are their
audience.

Bad Hair Life

Bad Hair Life

Chapter 11

One summer our whole
family attended the
Summer Institute of
Linguistics at the
University of Oklahoma.
My first class was on one
side of our dorm and
Alex's (my husband) class
was on the other. Our
second class was on his
side.

We had been notified they
were going to put a new

Bad Hair Life

hot top on the parking lot
that day, so we had all
moved our cars.

My class went overtime
and we were running to
get to the next class when
we encountered a five foot
wide strip of freshly poured
hot tar across the lot.

The men in the class
jumped over easily. I
sized it up, knowing I'd
never make it all the way
across, but thinking I could
just put one foot in the tar
and keep running.

Bad Hair Life

I took a running start,
revved up my engine and
ran as hard and jumped as
high as I could. I was
right. I didn't make it
across. Only both my feet
landed in the tar and
zipped out from under me,
laying me down in the
black stuff.

I was wearing a white
pants suit. My entire back
side from heel to hair was
coated with tar. I stood up
and announced to my
classmates, "I think I'll go
change clothes."

One of them assured me he would give my books to Alex.

Meantime when I was late for class Alex whispered to the fellow next to him, "If I know my wife, she's stuck in the tar."

The fellow didn't think that was too funny. Then my classmate came in and handed Alex my tar-spattered books. He whispered, "Your wife fell in the tar."

Bad Hair Life

The fellow next to Alex looked at him wide-eyed.

"I'm not a prophet, nor the son of a prophet. I just know my wife." Alex told him.

Back at the parking lot I held my hands straight out from my body and dripped tar as I waddled back to the dorm. I must have looked like a penguin with that white front and black back.

I managed to get some clean clothes and take

them to the hall bathroom. We didn't have private baths. I removed everything that had tar on it -- which was everything. I walked to the sink and turned on the water to wash my hands. The water just solidified the tar, but didn't remove one smidgen.

I stood there staring at my hands wondering what in the world I would do next. Another student walked in and screamed when she saw me.

Bad Hair Life

Can you imagine? I stood
there naked, with hair
plastered to the back of
my head.

She brought me a bottle of
olive oil and poured it into
my hands. That just rolled
the tar right off. She left
the bottle with me and I
went into the shower,
where I thoroughly
anointed myself with oil.

The only side effect was
that my hair (never oily
before) was oily for
months.

Bad Hair Life

Well, I guess you could
call it a side effect that
everyone on that campus
knew who I was. "You're
the lady who fell in the tar!"

Attention is fun – only not
when you're naked and
half tar-covered.

Chapter 12

Not only did I have hair problems, I was clumsy. Most of my life was decorated with a skinned knee. I even got married with a skinned knee. I had fallen off the <u>one</u> step from the chapel after the Wedding rehearsal.

If there is a hole or a bump anywhere around I'll fall in it or trip on it. Alex says I have the longest "falls" in history. I stumble clear

99

across a room trying to
catch my balance before
falling.

When I was sixteen
mouton coats were all the
rage. That is a fur made
from sheep. When it gets
wet it stinks like I imagine
a wet sheep smells.

On one of my dates with
Alex we were running to
church in the snow and, of
course, I slipped and fell
into a snow bank. My coat
was thoroughly
dampened, and it made
me and everyone who sat

around me very
uncomfortable with the
smell.

I sometimes tripped up the
curb and blackened my
eyes and broke my
glasses -- or bent them
into unbelievable
contortions.

One of my favorite stories
(I think from the Reader's
Digest) was of a debutant
ball where the girl was
being escorted down the
beautiful staircase after
being presented. She
tripped on her gown and

went tumbling all the way to the dance floor. Her escort went running after her and handed her a $10 bill, saying, "I never thought you'd do it."

That turned the horrified gasps of the audience into smiles and chuckles and relieved the girl of the embarrassment.

That guy became my hero!

Chapter 13

When we lived in Mexico
City our company provided
us with a Tennis Club
Membership as part of
Alex's salary package.
They offered massages
and beauty shop services.
I thought a massage
sounded great and the
cost was so small I bought
six months worth. This big
woman came in, dipped
her hands in oil and salt
and began trying to
remove all my skin! It was
awful. Then she showed

Bad Hair Life

me a huge poster of a lady
sumo wrestler.

"You're going to look just
like this if you don't quit
drinking Cokes," she told
me.

By the way, I didn't drink
Cokes. I drank Pepsi's.

I gave my massage
package to the next
woman I saw.

Then I tried the beauty
salon. I asked for a
permanent. I explained
that my hair would curl in

less than half the time of average hair, and it would frizz if left on the usual time. The operator appeared to understand me. Then put the solution on and left for lunch. I thought she would never return and I was sure I'd be bald headed when she finally rinsed that solution off.

It wasn't too bad, but I never went back to the Tennis Club -- for any reason.

Bad Hair Life

Probably my worst fall
happened in Mexico at the
border. We all jumped out
of the car to go to the
immigration office. My foot
got tangled in the seat belt
and I went out of the car
head first. I broke both
bones in my right forearm,
40% of my elbow, both
wrists, and tore the
meniscus in both knees.

I know how to do things in
a big way.

Chapter 14

Over time my hair became naturally streaked with gray. One day I was sitting in the chair getting a hair cut and watching women getting streaks of "blond" put into their darker hair. They were paying a lot of money to make their hair look like mine. Isn't God good? He saved me so much money by highlighting my hair for me.

Bad Hair Life

I watched women with
naturally curly hair spend
hours and tons of money
making their hair straight --
like mine. I like God's
way. It's cheaper and less
painful.

Another weird joke
happened as I aged. Hair
began to grow on my face.
-- not on my head! One
beauty shop "waxed" my
face and literally tore the
hair out. That was painful,
but it would be worth it, I
thought.

Bad Hair Life

Not so. Within days it grew back. Not only that, it grew back as whiskers -- tough and prickly. I was going to France on a business trip (that's why I submitted to the torture) and I wanted to be beardless. By the time we arrived the hair had grown back and every European gave me cheek kisses and shied away from my whiskers.

Since my facial hair is white, I decided it was better soft and white than hard and prickly!

Bad Hair Life

Skin cancer became
prevalent with people in
the news. I could
remember as a teenager
lying in the sun and putting
baby oil and iodine on
myself to make a tan. I'd
burn myself badly. I can
even remember having the
part in my hair swell with
the burn.

I went to a dermatologist
to have myself checked
and to have some pre-
cancerous spots removed.

Bad Hair Life

Because I was worried
about skin cancer he
suggested I apply a topical
chemo therapy. It would
burn out any diseased
cells, but not hurt the
healthy cells.

I applied it twice a day
over my entire face.
Before long 75% of my
face became 3rd degree
burns. The scabs cracked
when I spoke, or smiled or
ate.

When the scabs fell off
one of my granddaughters
told me, "Grandma, your

Bad Hair Life

face doesn't look like a
tiger anymore."

The doctor told me with
my fair skin and thin hair it
would be foolish for me to
go out in the sun without
covering my head.

If I had to cover my head,
and my hair didn't do that,
it meant I needed to wear
hats.

HATS!

Why didn't I think of that solution years earlier?

Talk about fancy! This is
one of my hats I call the
Queen Elizabeth style .

I don't know what to call

this one.

Bad Hair Life

Chapter 15

Hats by Teri Hoover

My mother has a
reputation of being the
lady in the hat
A mover and shaker in her
own right,
knowing where it's at.
Hats are an extension of
your personality
But we all must keep up
the reality.
A hat must be worn and
chosen
with care.
When it comes down to it
Hats just cover up your
hair!

Bad Hair Life

Hats originally were
used for protection. '
They were functional. I
rather imagine Adam
and Eve used one of
their fig leaves to cover
their heads to protect
them from the sun.
Since rain hadn't been
invented, they didn't
need it for that reason.

Nomadic people didn't
wear hats, but they
covered their heads with
cloth for protection.

Bad Hair Life

Hats became symbols of authority. Kings and leaders wore crowns. The Pope and Cardinals wear symbolic head gear. Chieftains wore animal skins. Our Native Americans wore feathers, but only after they earned that right. The number and kind of feathers denoted rank or accomplishment.

Bad Hair Life

Masai Leader's hat.

Early jesters wore silly
hats to symbolize their
station in life.

Military men wear helmets
and caps, all embossed
with their rank.

Bad Hair Life

Construction workers wear
hard hats.

Cowboys wear sombreros
not only to protect
themselves from sun, rain,
wind and dust, (and birds)
but they used their hats to
scoop up water and drink
from it. That's disgusting!

After living where water
was not plentiful, and
being unable to wash my
hair daily, I learned the
probable reason women
long ago began wearing
hats – to cover up bad
hair.

I found 16 pages on Google for hats. Most of those sites were selling hats, but I found some interesting facts. We commonly refer to the good guys as the guys in "white" hats. Teachers tell their students to put on their "thinking" hats. Years ago, the misbehaving child got to sit in the corner wearing a "dunce" hat. I'm glad today that's "old hat."

We have "party" hats, stocking hats, tams, and turbans.

Bad Hair Life

There was a time when no
woman would attend
church without a hat. In
many countries that is still
true. Wealthy women in
Europe and even in
America in earlier times
kept their skin covered and
protected from the sun.
I'm not sure when that
concept changed to be
replaced with tanning
booths. I guess people
just go from one extreme
to another.

Only in the 1960's did the
hat become less

123

fashionable, and the
millinery shops closed.
Now only a few die-hard
hat-wearers still exist.

This die-hard has a
healthy collection of such.

I certainly don't want to be
"talking through my hat," in
telling you baseball hats
have a huge place in the
advertising world today.
You can find company
logos, sayings, and jokes
embroidered on ball caps.
Our kids gave this ball cap
to Alex for Christmas. It
sent a message.

Bad Hair Life

Bad Hair Life

I used to love hats when I
was little. My mother
wouldn't have dreamed of
going to town shopping
without a hat and gloves. I
remember window
shopping at the many
millenary stores. You
could choose a model;
they would measure your
head and make the hat to
exactly fit.

Sometime before I got to
the age to wear those
beautiful hats they went
out of style. We only wore
hats on Easter.

Now they don't make hats
in sizes for women. They
say "one size fits all" but
they don't! I have some
hats that fall down over my
ears. And one sits on top
of my head so that if the
wind blows it goes
tumbling down the street.

I tried to make them fit, but had little luck. Then I decided to take my problem to a men's hat store. I know they block men's hats and make them fit.

Bad Hair Life

Isn't it funny there are
shops that make custom
hats and boots for men,
but not for women. Men's
clothing stores alter their
clothes to fit, but not many
stores will alter women's
clothes.

The owner of the men's
hat store suggested I go to
a hardware store and buy
some insulation strips
used on R.V.'s to glue
inside my hat band. I did
that.

Problem with that was
when I took the hat off, my

Bad Hair Life

hair stuck to the insulation
more than it stuck to the
hat, and it pulled out my
hair. I couldn't afford that.
I discarded the tape.

Bad Hair Life

Bad Hair Life

Chapter 17

If I had to wear hats, I
might as well have fun with
it. I had inherited some
hats from my mother so I
started with those. As I
wore them, people began
to say, "I can't wear hats,
but I have a neat one.
Would you like to have it?"

Of course I would. On
birthdays and
anniversaries or Mothers'
Day my family bought

Bad Hair Life

hats. Friends bought me
hats. To date I own more
than sixty. I love them.
And still I buy them when I
find a bargain or one of a
color I don't have.

I began with a cloth hat
with a conservative bill.
Then I got bolder.

One hat was given to me
from Africa. It looks like
one of those sun shields
you put in the car window.
It is made of two hoops of
wire covered in a red silk
material. When you
stretch it over your head

each hoop pops up in a
different direction. It gets
a lot of attention -- and I
like attention.

Bad Hair Life

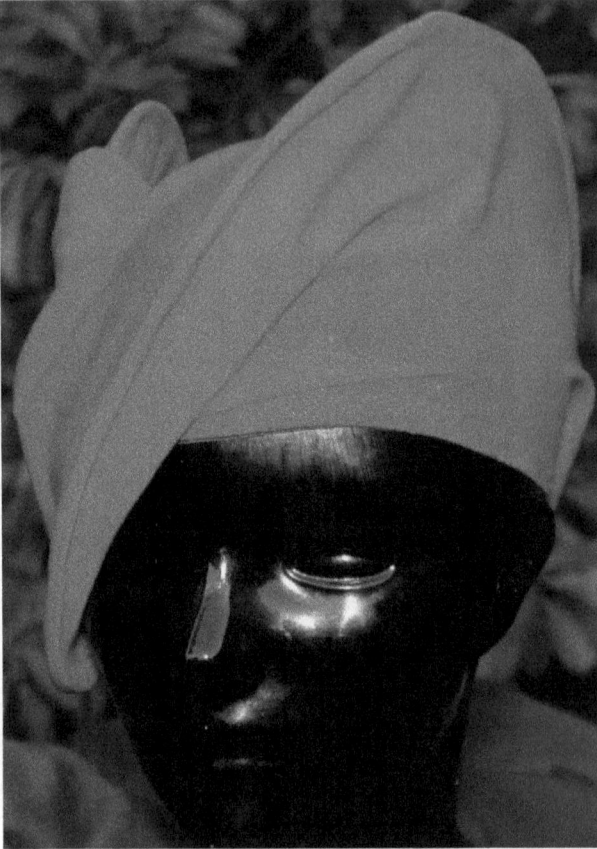

Some hats are fancier

than others. My mood for

Bad Hair Life

the day predicts what I
choose to wear.

I have fancy "Queen
Elizabeth" type hats, and
biker hats. Mostly I wear
conservative toppers.
People don't recognize me
when I'm not wearing a
hat.

Bad Hair Life

My prize hat belonged to
my grandmother. It is a
black "picture" hat with a
wide brim of net with wool
felt leaves sewn on it. It
has ostrich feathers across
the top. I have worn it a
couple of times, but the
net is so fragile that it tears
easily. Now that hat sits
on a black glass head on a
shelf in my office.

I have a picture of my
grandmother wearing the
hat, but she is also
wearing a Groucho Marx
nose and glasses. She

Bad Hair Life

was a laffologist before
me.

I have another picture of
my mother wearing the
hat. She was also wearing
one of my after five
dresses and men's socks.
She won the "tacky" party
award. I don't know which
was more insulting – my
dress winning or that
beautiful hat.

Bad Hair Life

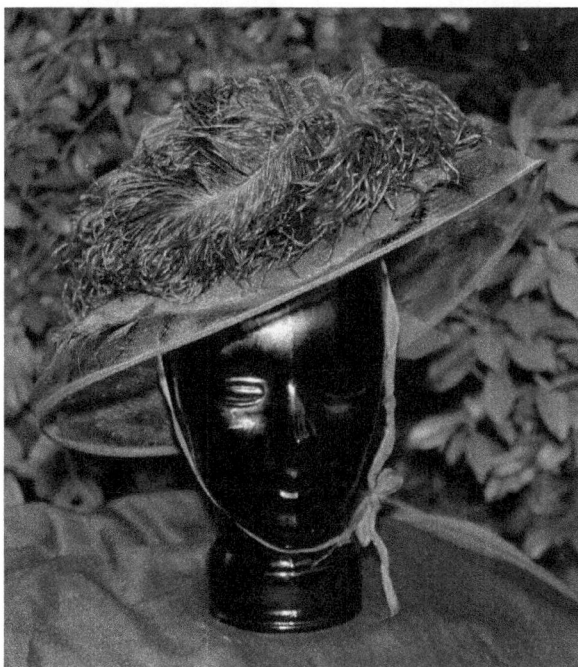

Bad Hair Life

I wore the ostrich feather
hat when I played the part
of Susanna Wesley, the
mother of John and
Charles Wesley. It was a
satire on Samuel Wesley,
her husband. I'm sure
Susanna never wore such
a fancy hat, since she was
reared as a Puritan and
was kept too poor by her
husband to afford anything
fancy. Not only that, she
had something like 17
children.

Biker hats are fun.

I bought this vase from a
show in Branson, Missouri.

Derby

The accordian paper of the vase, when
stretched over your head makes a cute
derby hat. And when it is stretched
over the other way it makes you look
like a Monopoly Piece.

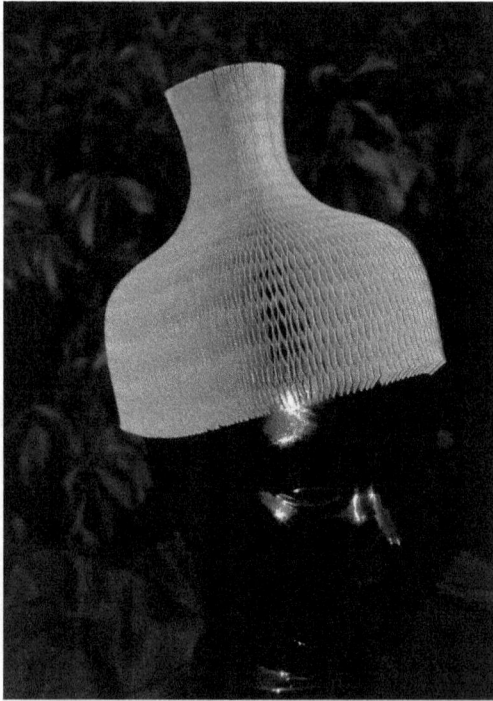

Monopoly Piece hat

Chapter 17

Alex went to South
America on business and
his colleague took him to a
hat store where they sold
Panama Hats. He
convinced Alex to buy one
for $150. He assured Alex
the hat would be worth
$500 at least in the U.S.
We moved several times
after that and the hat got
all crumpled up. We were
invited to a Murder

Mystery Dinner and were
encouraged to dress the
part. I took the wrinkled
up hat to a well known hat
store to be blocked.

A week passed and the
hat wasn't ready. Another
week passed and we went
in to check on it. The clerk
brought it out, but it had
been torn. We were
shocked. The store owner
came out to see what was
happening. When he saw
the damage and knew it
was the fault of his
employee, he reached to a
shelf and brought down an

identical Monte Cristo Panama Hat – with a price tag of $1500 on it. He handed it to Alex.

Although the hat was identical to our original it was a smaller size and was not comfortable for Alex to wear. So I have inherited the most expensive hat I've ever seen.

Bad Hair Life

Another of my hat stories
took place on my first
mountain climbing
adventure.

Alex and I were still in language
school when we had a break
and drove to Chihuahua to
choose a village to make our
home.

The morning we headed for our
first real mountain adventure, I
dressed carefully while it was
still dark. I wanted to look my
best as the new missionary. I
wore a red and white print dress,
a matching red sombrero – tied
in place against the wind, panty

hose and practically new orthopedic shoes.

I dressed like I thought a good missionary would dress.

We drove as far as the truck was able to navigate the trails, then we walked to the edge of a cliff and looked down into a village below. The basketball court looked the size of a postage stamp.

Then we had to walk down from our approximately 9,000 feet altitude to about

Bad Hair Life

3,000 feet. The trail was
covered with dry pine
needles and loose rocks.

I fell so many times I lost
count, but usually I landed
on my well padded bottom.
In one spot the loose rocks
slipped out from under my
feet and I tumbled forward
making a complete
somersault -- landing with
my hat in place!

By the time we finally
reached the village I was
covered with fine grey
dust; my hose were
shredded; my knees were

bleeding; my dress was
torn and I was being
supported by my son on
one side and a walking
stick on the other. I had
no control of my legs. I'd
tell my foot to step over a
rock, but it wouldn't. I
stumbled into the village.

They voted to let us live
there, especially the little
old grandmother (And I
was not a grandmother
then.)

They promised to make a
burro trail for me to get
into the village, but noted

the rains would wash out
the trail each year. We
unanimously voted NOT to
live there.

By the way, those
practically new orthopedic
shoes never again walked
on flat ground. They were
permanently worn off at
the slant of the mountain.

This photo is of Mae speaking as a world
famous
novel writer – Mother Goose.

Bad Hair Life

Chapter 19

I was asked to perform a
spoof on a world famous
novel writer. I dressed the
part and took a gaudy bag
of props to show how the
writer has to be prepared
for any event or accident
while traveling.

The speech was at the
Ridglea Country Club. As
I strolled across the busy
lobby of the Club a
number of people passed
me without a single

comment or second look.
It made me wonder what
their regular membership
was like.

Following my performance
I was driving home and
within a few blocks of my
home I failed to stop my
car BEFORE the stop sign
and failed to make a right
turn signal before turning.
A policeman pulled me
over.

My wallet with driver's
license was at the bottom
of my prop bag. I had to

Bad Hair Life

get out of the car and dig
down to find it.

I explained my costume as
I pulled out some rather
embarrassing props, such
as orange bikini panties
and a water pistol. (You
do have to be prepared.)

The officer took my license
back to his patrol car to
check me out and I got
back in my car, chuckling
over my predicament. He
returned and handed me
my license.

"I'm going to give you a warning this time, Mrs. Hoover." He extended his hand for a shake. "And it's been a pleasure meeting you."

After changing clothes my husband and I drove to the store and passed the place where I had been stopped. The officer was gone. I'll bet he hurried back to the precinct and told his fellow officers, "You'll never guess who I just stopped!"

Bad Hair Life

Another of my regular gigs
is during a business
course at Knowledge for
Success.

When the subject of
networking to build your
business is presented, I
come in usually wearing
overalls with one leg rolled
up, my husband's black
socks and house slippers,
chewing gum, handing out
dirty business cards with
the phone number marked
out and another one
written in, and talking
loudly on the cell phone.
I'm rude and don't listen to

the students when they try
to tell me what their
business is. Sometimes
they want to throw me out
of the room.

Then I leave, change into
a business suit and return
with my brief case.

The students are able to
talk about all the negative
impressions I left, and I
explain that I have actually
seen people at network
events doing just as badly
as I had done.

Bad Hair Life

I have a lot of fun and
when they realize I'm not
for real, they get a laugh
with me.

Bad Hair Life

Chapter 20

Hair wasn't the only
problem I had staying in
fashion. As a teenager --
in the pre-panty hose days
-- we wore girdles with
little clippy deals to hold up
the nylon stockings.
Those were uncomfortable
and usually rolled at the
waist, causing misery.

Playtex came out with a
rubber girdle and I went

with my Aunt Lena to buy
one for herself. She was
fat. I waited outside the
dressing room while the
clerk helped Aunt Lena get
the garment on. Then
Lena began screaming. I
hurried to see what was
happening. The girdle
was rolling itself into her
rolls of fat and had already
made several rolls before
she started screaming. I
thought we were going to
have to cut it off her or
maybe operate, but the
clerk managed with my
help to free Lena. I

determined never to buy
one of those.

Then some brilliant person
designed panty hose. I
was overweight and
considered myself to be
fat. I went to the
department store and
bought three pairs of extra
large hose.

That night we were going
out and I was to take the
kids to the baby sitter. I
put on a pair of my new
hose. By the time I got to
the front door of the house

they had begun to gather around my ankles.

I pulled the waist up as high as I could and smoothed the wrinkles back up my legs. By the time I got to the car my ankles were bundles of wrinkles. I took off my shoes and pulled the excess material under my foot, put the shoes back on and continued to the sitter.

When I arrived at the sitter I again had puddles of wrinkles. Again I removed

Bad Hair Life

my shoes and pulled the
excess material under my
foot, and clear to my heel.

When I got home I took
the things off and held
them up. They were taller
than I was.

The next day I took the
extra pairs back to the
store and proudly
announced, "These are
too big for me!" Boy was
that fun!

In those beginning days of
panty hose they made
them with actual feet -- not

the tubes like we have
today.

I put on a new pair and in
a few minutes I noticed the
heel of one of the
stockings was on top of
my foot instead of under it.
I took them off and turned
them around. Then the
heel was on top of the
other foot. I took them off
and examined them. They
had been woven with one
foot facing one way and
the other facing the other
way.

Bad Hair Life

The clerk and I both got a
laugh out of that one.

Tube panty hose solved
that problem.

When I was a school
teacher one morning I was
in the teachers' lounge
drinking coffee when the
speech therapist came in.
I noticed the heels of her
hose were on top of her
ankles. I pointed it out to
her.

She looked down,
shrugged and said, "You
should see my bra. I put it

on backwards this morning. Now people can't see if I'm coming or going."

As teachers of elementary school we usually wore pants so we could get down with the kids. One morning that same therapist came in wearing a dress.

"Are you going to a funeral? Is that why you're wearing a dress?"

"No," she answered, "I'm wearing a dress because I

shaved my legs and didn't want to waste it."

I always hated when I put on new hose and popped a runner before I even got out the door. I went on and wore them. If anyone noticed I would act surprised and say, "My goodness, just look at that!" They'd think it just happened. If I was going to different groups of people I could get away with that for several wears before having to throw them out.

Bad Hair Life

My best friend was a professional model. She was 5 foot 7 inches tall and weighed about 100 pounds. She was going shopping one day and I asked if I could go along. She said, "Sure, but the store I go to won't carry your size."

Well, I went anyway. I found one dress that fit. (I only thought I was fat -- well, and my friend thought I was, too). It wouldn't have mattered what that dress looked like -- I bought it. Actually it was

Bad Hair Life

pretty cute and I wore it for
several years.

Until I really got fat.

Speaking of fat, I keep my
digital scales three pounds
heavy. That way when I
step on and read the
meter I can say, "I don't
really weigh that much!"

I was teaching sixth grade
and because of the air
conditioning I always wore
a jacket. One day the air
was off and I took my
jacket off.

Bad Hair Life

One of my students asked,
"Mrs. Hoover, why don't
you wear sleeveless
blouses more often?"

"It's usually cold in here.
Why do you ask?"

"We just like it so we can
watch your arms jiggle
when you write on the
board."

Another time I was
teaching first grade and
had playground duty. I
took my jacket off in the
heat.

Bad Hair Life

One of my students came
up and said, "Mrs. Hoover,
my mama has a pants suit
just like yours." He
hesitated a moment before
adding, "And hers is too
tight, too."

If you can't stand the truth,
don't ever work with kids.

I used to make my own
clothes. I had one
particular dress I really
liked, so I kept it for years.
Alex accepted the
pastorate of a church. I
wore that dress one
Sunday morning.

Bad Hair Life

An elderly lady came up
and asked, "Did you make
that dress, Mae?"

"Why yes," I answered
proudly.

"You just hang on to it and
it will come right back into
style,"

Old people are just as
truthful as little children.

I put the dress in Good
Will.

Bad Hair Life

The parsonage was next
door to the church, but
there was almost the
length of a football field
between the two. I was
accustomed to wearing
pants to teach first grade.
At that time women didn't
wear pants to church. I
almost froze walking to
church in short skirts, so I
made long skirts to match
each of my pairs of pants.
I wore the long skirts over
the pants to keep warm.

My mother (who was
always fashion conscious
and frustrated because I

Bad Hair Life

wasn't) said, "Mae, long
skirts are not in style."

"Mother," I said, "In my
church I make the style."

Sure enough before long
all the women were
wearing long skirts – over
their pants.

Now before you start
feeling sorry for me and
my bad hair, just think ... If
I hadn't had bad hair --
what would I have to write
a book about?

And besides ... I have sixty
really cute hats!   And a
couple of empty wig
heads.

And besides ... I have
plenty of stories to make
myself a "Laffologist,"
making people laugh.

About the Author

Mae Hoover is a speaker, an author of seven books, and founder/director of Foundation for Publication, teaching and guiding beginning writers through the process of producing, publishing and promoting their own book.

Contact Mae to book her to speak or to enroll in the program.

http://FoundationForPublication.com
817 229 4895
info@FoundationForPublication.com

This book is filled with stories about the "fashion" catastrophes in Mae's life – all of which she found reason to laugh about – eventually.

She gets great joy over making people laugh, and she has done so all her life.

To book Mae as a speaker for your event call (817) 229 4895 or email mae@maehoover.com. Website www:TheLadyInTheHat.com

Mae and Alex after 56
years of marriage

Published by Mountain

Top Books

A division of Foundation

for Publication

Fort Worth, TX 76133

Copyrighted 2013-08-01

ISBN 978-0-9962717-1-4

Bad Hair Life

www.ingramcontent.com/pod-product-compliance
Lightning Source LLC
Chambersburg PA
CBHW060443040426
42331CB00044B/2513